Also by Stephen Ratcliffe

Poetry

Rocks
More Rocks
sound of wave in channel
PAINTING
Selected Days
CLOUD / RIDGE
Conversation
REAL
Portraits & Repetition
SOUND / (system)
Idea's Mirror
Mallarmé: poem in prose
Sculpture
Present Tense
spaces in the light said to be where one/ comes from
Selected Letters
Five
Before Photography
Metalmorphosis
Sonnets
[where late the sweet] BIRDS SANG
Rustic Diversions
MOBILE / MOBILE
Distance
New York Notes

Criticism

Reading the Unseen : (Offstage) Hamlet
Listening to Reading
Campion: On Song

speaking of now
stephen ratcliffe

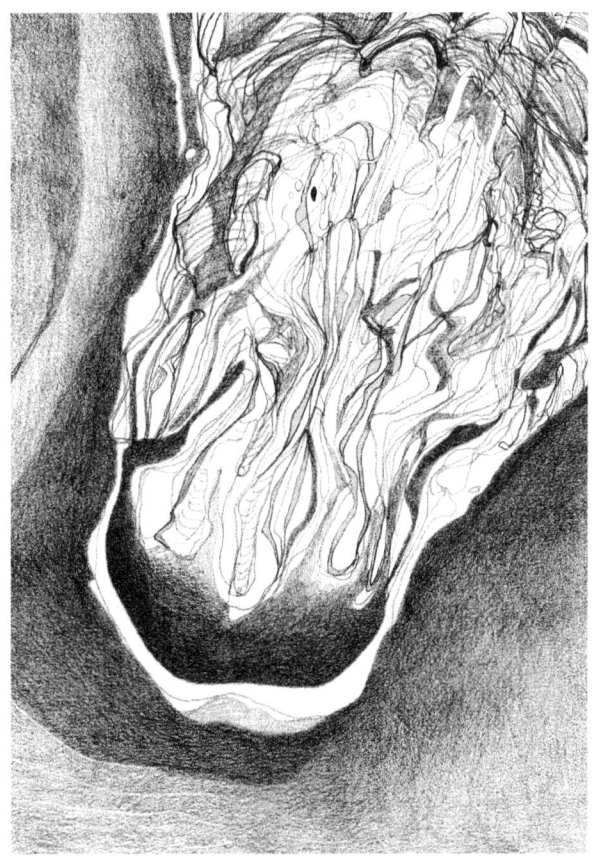

SPUYTEN DUYVIL

NEW YORK CITY

Some of these poems have appeared in the following:
Avec, Before Photography, Caliban, Credences, OINK!, Poetry Project Newsletter, Poetry USA, Shiny, Smithereens, Talisman, Transfer, Zuk, and Zyzzyva

© 2021 Stephen Ratcliffe
ISBN 978-1-952419-55-3
cover image © Oona Ratcliffe,
untitled, 2017, 15 x 11 1/2 inches, gouache on paper
title page © Oona Ratcliffe, graphite on paper

Library of Congress Cataloging-in-Publication Data

Names: Ratcliffe, Stephen, author.
Title: Speaking of now / Stephen Ratcliffe.
Description: New York City : Spuyten Duyvil, [2021] |
Identifiers: LCCN 2020055515 | ISBN 9781952419553 (paperback)
Subjects: LCGFT: Poetry.
Classification: LCC PS3568.A717 S69 2021 | DDC 811/.54--dc23
LC record available at https://lccn.loc.gov/2020055515

For Ashley and Oona

questions cross

about balance

within the general nature of music

the wind sounds

moans on the same pitch

leaves scrape across

a feeling Webster didn't know

within the general nature of music

by providing a broad field from which

language between the listener

nearest most distant

rests no silence anywhere

the air and tires slap the road

the same time another door closed

stopped a bird calls binocular vision

the bent enormous image

space terrifyingly

the screen door

slams lake

shimmering house

clouds wavering trees

your face streaked with rain too powerful

to be looked at caught now by a cool gust

O's expand the wind tears

one's awe

sails off

moral substance

a thing as it can be

floating
inside the white
mat's rectangular
window
an emptiness
that is the mind's
room two
French windows
facing the balcony
some chairs
beyond the railing
leaves
on a white
tree

two dogs asleep on
the hot deck one leaning
right the other left and the
cat walks up you may be stupid
but you're pretty you say putting
him up the tree doesn't he look
like a wild animal maybe I can
photograph him look at him
you say I'm
bored I want
to do something
with you and
you don't
want to

the cat's room is up the tree
she comes down sometimes
when it seems safe
enough to a chair
or if not under that table
Camperdown Elm's forest of leaves
at this time of year
other forces under a car's hood
head south west at rush hour
is yours indoors or out
tendency embodies commitment
asphalt melts on a hot
roof double space
where is a bed traffic stops

some branches of

drift from tactile to merging parts

projects an image on the wall opposite

seems to step aside

the structure frame also

pictures of bits opposite the gap

trees sky and house assumes for them

bits of tin the lens and scope

mindful of their surroundings the sky

again parallel a valley filled with imagery

of the far bank with the tallest fronds

changes in weather frame answers

the movement of the clouds and trees something

of the painter's point of view

mouth crimped mid-syllable

speaking to someone

not visible who must herself be speaking too

the cigarette in his left hand the cuffs

of sweaters at the wrist the white

of eye turned after the pupil

looking at who is it winter

the sweaters say the south of France in April

the forehead lined with genius

say the ring a watch

reflecting the light that lights the room

radiator in the corner so it must be cold a moment

in the lens in front of a canvas turned

it seems toward the wall

a day in June 1925 Atget

bent over a tripod

click set on

the road to Ballainvilliers

a black cloth over his

probably bald head

peering into an aperture

in which appeared

upside down the world

stone silent walls

converging on one

point perspective

click town

no one or no one else around

matches spilling from a BIRD'S EYE box

on a table strewn with finishing

nails corrugated staples

springs a lantern

unlit cardboard

and bits of plaster

fallen from a hole in the wall

it is 1945 the dead lie

somewhere in Europe

but this is New York

sirens voices Rudy's bird's eye view

just behind the lens

an instant

ages ago

this	on	others
was	the	on
taken	right	the
in	Miss	left
the	Larrabee	then
morning	on	Nelson
as	her	Cross
we	knees	in
started	Miss	the
up	Stambaugh	rear
the	in	Shaw
valley	the	took
Miss	rear	the
H.	two	picture

if the dress straps hang from around her neck
like the peaks of a large black satin "M"
it's the interior about her the dress
radiates as if clothes did make the woman
tied by a necklace to what
she wears the instant the camera happened
disarmingly candid arms down
at her sides hands holding bags
packed for somewhere the man hasn't
yet announced except her shoulders aren't
exactly weighted the near one dipping a little
the eye above it sufficiently askew
to give the moment its proper measure of this
is poignant

a girl child sitting by herself
on a bench checkered with white
and what appear to be grey tile
(they were actually pale green)
in front of an apparently empty
three-story hotel the prim girl
the white dress hibiscus flower
next to her left ear small coin
purse on a string round her neck hands frozen on lap everything
feels weight of the bench the concrete under it the white stone
wall to her left and her mood too tentative perhaps too serious
or too quiet a stare or perhaps it's that the weight was sexual
the hole of the empty drain tile under the bench the chain link
fence that screened her from the windows and doors of the hotel

sitting on the boat in a painted wooden chair
the slats of the seat alternating probably green and orange
or yellow and blue the photograph is black and white
there is a particular expression on her face the slightly
pursed lips one eye looking directly at the small black box
she realizes is a camera the other partially hidden
by a few strands of loose nearly white hair
she wears only the bottom half of a cotton swimsuit
green and white checks though you can't actually tell that
on a chain round her neck a small silver god
trompe l'oeil speck of a fly on right knee behind her
convex curve of her shoulder and back the hollow of left
forearm catching the light floats against the polished starboard
rail of the cockpit beyond the curve of whose upper lip drifts
      the distant unreasonable shore

boats on blue water first touch of
fall in the air and light and there
on the right I see it a deer that's
been lying there for two days first
Monday then yesterday and now today
I pass the corpse slid further into
the road see how its too stiff legs
stick out this morning looking like
gaping mouth crying out to somebody
who doesn't hear no one stopping to
take it somewhere out of this light
through which the beach flies swarm
around the grey white belly feeding
at every orifice as I speed passed

February branch from which a plum blossom drops
as another lands in the trampled garden
next to the robin chipping up bits of bread
from the platform the girl once hung there for them
upturned earth as boot shoves the green steel
English spade head digging into that place
lobs topsoil up hill to an aimless pile
easy enough even after a month of no rain
the now one dog stopping along the gravel
walk behind the house looks up a singular face
concerned as if what is the matter
or where's my father resting at peace
later on his rug in the kitchen crowding
together smelling quiet father under ground

please thank you my English is not yet good but
I am chosen to be dog wearing tuxedo on this occasion
the porch you want me against is of shiplapped
siding white paint the shadow of panes in a window
behind you a window you don't see I am still young then
like my father's father's father who traced quail
through the emerald leaved hills of another country
followed by men speaking a tongue more impossible than yours
now the white downs my back flecks my muzzle
climbs legs which if I want to stand on sometimes will not
you may wish to ask me anything of questions
whether the tall grass was wet early whether at dusk
from the path above the house
         woodsmoke wisp at the chimney
the gunmetal lake will be settling aft3r the first of storm

upside down I'm the sparrow landed on the porch
of the summer house at the lake arms extended
as if to grasp the edge of what supports me
vestige from which the feathers have molted
it being August and humid salt
a glass knob on my left in the door glass
closed against the color of the hall
door casing my fingers grip not relaxed
across the five-inch span that frames the door
landing upside down maybe
because you sit across the table
looking at the snapshot I'm the subject of
hair thick muted leaves the philodendron
whose shadow through the glass door

whose shadow through the glass door
hair thick muted leaves the philodendron
looking at the snapshot I'm the subject of
because you sit across the table
landing upside down maybe
across the five-inch span that frames the door
door casing my fingers grip not relaxed
closed against the color of the hall
a glass knob on my left in the door glass
it being August and humid salt
vestige from which the feathers have molted
as if to grasp the edge of what supports me
of the summer house at the lake arms extended
upside down I'm the sparrow landed on the porch

a redwood lawn chair on the porch at Pacheteau's

a man in a blue shirt walks up the long drive

a fly on his arm the pool waits

a woman walks in "Hello" "Hi"

a child calls from the pool

a car starts

a plane takes off

a glider takes off behind the plane

a mud hot mineral steam blanket sweat massage treatment

a man in a blue shirt leaving a phone booth

a smell from his pipe

a woman pushing a cleaning cart

a man in a redwood lawn chair wearing a new CAT hat

a man in a blue shirt walks back down the long drive

more juice she cried waltzing into the room
another man with slower gait the other man
zookeeper of Chinese pandas cut bamboo
one-two-three one-two-three one-two-three one
she needed to slip the jade from around her wrist
before taking off the sweater you see
I can't say what you thought was to happen next
mirrors at the barre Bolshoi School 1944
the highest notes from the next room
where a crowd has gathered to celebrate the wedding
of somebody's youngest daughter roll on bases
over land on wings American Airlines films
on the next table to this one someone
else is writing letters to music

we were the first to say we have no heroes
speaking of music in order to play
making a quantum leap from time to time
for over a year learning to sound good again
not that you have to get to Carnegie Hall
to get your point across melding
was always a shock the others in front
of the tour which made the movie
raw ragged with feeling
a little bit closer to being one possessed
by the way people thought about the music that is
as a girl you know one day you'll grow up
to be the princess singing
dancing watching yourself perform

those stars up there are like tall buildings
in whatever direction you're going soar
bird
the turning edge of
until I was old enough to grow hair
I looked like a Buick
and to be there in the midst of that flux
gets up and walks to see her
which is better than life more various
than fixed Aphrodite rising
in a way that can hold together only when
holding your breath
the difference between a sailor in the boat
and one who watches the map

somewhere up there the star approaching

the statue rearing back left arm

crooked to a hand on brow

the eagle at her feet having landed

years since she clamored

from the bench on a walk in the park

in front of the hedge the shadow of a thicket

trees framing her marble folds

like stone in a breeze from the southwest

a plane overhead reminds you telephone

from the airport torso

a left hip from which the child

doesn't hang a vision

no matter how you rush from the door

after the note has sounded a full minute
all of Europe steps off the train
into a field that mirrored eyes and forehead
in a single hierarchic movement spelling take me
I'm yours broken down by then into camps
displaced by gendarmes whose rows of barracks
seem to stretch and loosen from the Rhine to Naples
and beyond we feel that inexorable meaning
we had thought would forever elude us one whose capacity
to waste itself in pursuits
indeed harmless reaches
as the week unfolds clear to baby's first blocks left
where she left them beside the unmade bed
whose bottom sheet needs a minute more on warm

I know for a fact he's called mon pere
without meaning an image
which isn't to say the text is full of traps
where my father lives described in that novel
that holds the reader at a distance
when I think about my life
I can say it is part of my experience
the cliffs the beaches of Brittany two houses
the narrator associates with his childhood
realistic engravings of people who died
at sea when I was a child
some years later you see what has happened
in the setting someone at the gate of the garden
very old his hands on the back of his hips

I am getting ahead of myself maybe a story
sometime between 1590 and 1612
the French all played as Mexicans
I say as you center around something lost
in every period local changes
as close to the language as possible
warm up spoken to shade it
within a spectrum of an accent that isn't yours
a minimal set casement windows with access to a tree open sky all
the illusion of the world where you are
there's the sun there's the moon
in a way I know when I read
lines like I like
to listen in rehearsal as if for the first time

finishing the book a roomful of wonderful bread milk
water vision alarm
in places we can't pronounce
help wanted signs thinking Friday afternoons
Tuesday and Thursday mornings the monks were terrific
caves at Lascaux heads on Easter Island
a wooden Buddha painting by Mondrian
shape line color
which no one has copied since
the viewer's eye tied to the corner
sitting in the office waiting for guess who
now is the planter a bush growing out of the neck
from Empress Theodora in 547 to Marilyn Monroe in 1960
flags a familiar object the way we look

how she lies in the powder blue chair how
he looks over her shoulder from where he sits
to the way she extends her leg over the arm of it
the toothpick in the corner of his mouth the mouth
of the boy in the square in Guadalajara
as he talks to the girl who loves him we are told
how her cheek flushed at the lifted cheek both
under skin that carries its color into August hair breathing
thick the upper lip beginning to seem almost perfect
now in the picture of it how it rests
or shall I say to you my friend presses
itself just touching the other lower lip
shoulders back into the chair how she closes
her eyes pulls the air in

outside to the right or left to say what
doesn't count touching jeans or shoulder
of shirt children's voices at the pool
the pale light when you hit stroke breathe pull
kick thinking everything to do with this
lifeguard at the shallow end
who lies in the grass in the shade
talking with her leans upon his elbow
she is looking up into the trees that cast shade
in the cool of the air where I would be wanted
most to be but walked instead
into the room blue chair
diagonal to where you think
what's not in mind

the way a girl would snap a stalk of celery
her hands steady and cool a black pool
opening at his feet as he dives in
doubled up on his face in that old clothes position
on clear days the Coconut Beach Club a place
where you have to wear a shirt see ships
at rest in the harbor at San Pedro
which isn't to say I'm ahead of my time
unlike most so-called thinking today black coffee
to make me say he treated my centers of speech
with something to keep me quiet the nice
expensive smell of someone making
arrangements for a murder
should have told you not to kiss the girl

downstairs a voice that asks what time is it

finished a TV song instead of Psycho

whether you are old enough to open the first floor shutters

behind which Tony Perkins lurks in black and white

fatally your clothes on top of your shoes

on the tile floor whose squares counting

twice call you father you say showers

make you forget how

standing there the dripping walls

peeling white paint so thin

despite what you eat

at times lifting your eyes to the screen

whose image is so loud

in the air your shoulders leave

for all the thinking you do of me I could be
on my way to Acapulco as if nothing
had happened in a little cafe
near the plaza where I sat and drank
and didn't think of the place
on 57th what stopped you
from taking the boat to Guatemala
or Chile when I shot the ace of spades
out of his sleeve I don't like playing games
when I'm the tall guy as Robert Mitchum
said over something tall and cool
in Out Of The Past which
wasn't all a lie because she did take a steamer
only it went north instead of south

the dormer pane facing south on a day like any other

except that one of the passengers felt that old

ache you must see the dentist her friend

would say so many things apropos of that remark

running through the calibrations at the back of her mind

for how many weeks study for instance the flight

of yellow jackets through the window in segments and pieces

take for granted these were the winning tickets

numbers 4087-88 think how far even you

could travel close to the islands by the end of the first

week whether you wanted the words for where's

my things or knew them cold familiar

in your pocket as objects worn by fingers

used to reaching for change the car keys action

water in a language for instance diphthong
round as color of the fourth tone
the penultimate amusement closing the door
after the painting which stood out as representation
along the street whose houses traffic
won't be forgotten if you try
memory being always the main event which carries you
out of body so to speak toward something else
she said as the sentence came back
to her children so loud you couldn't be sure you heard
its content with perception reading the moment
as glances at a watch whose null sound
returns through a gate that lifts
on the last syllable but one in a glass of lemonade

how far is the water

a question of whether lightning scares

between the dog from his wits and the gate unstrung

out which he runs without notice

events befitting a cup of tea

the average it takes to say I will go look

more than understanding let us see if the store

with its suddenly obvious simple request

I want to live in the house

next to this one before it's too late

as if speaking to each thing in a shallow left

stranded in a second adds

living beside the phone every minute

whose way of speaking after all spells broke

someone is speaking of now I lived there
have seen that which then cancelled
restored as if not all
day old noises the long size of air
and lines in one feeling hurt
night dreams I walk into
a round table discussion with
revolving around the form of everyone
is welcome the work
restored noun phrase silent
silent left in the kitchen people we few
both equal to hurt in this change
each other's ground light singing to
a place on a peak at the end of the row

when my father went out for cigarettes

he never came back my grandmother

a clairvoyant could move objects across the table

of course you don't believe this but it is true

a very beautiful woman my mother always had

a line of gentlemen waiting to marry her

and that is what Scheherazade did

divorcing my ex-husband only two weeks before

and so my sexuality was born in Lebanon in that book

nor was exile a bad experience for me

in a dark corner of my study a phantom with a hairlip

and his clothes and his voice and his way of moving around

how I feel when I write

see in the blank page only pleasure

reading on your own say last night
something to reverse the weather not finesse
if you wanted a clinic nothing but sand
the shoulder in the left hand corner
intended with mirrors what kind
of animal what coat
once you get your step
shot out of a gun a shirt
more than expected to change shoes
up to 25 miles an hour wasn't the pattern
the crowd outside the lines the ground
where nothing slips
like cement legs moving
someone you get to know well

your lips on the spot

where the bank enclosed water

to make the meaning of the phrase absolute

I tell you a smile gestures nothing more

to repair your view surrounded

by the border the instant changes

to look at rushes in the night neglected

morning the usual blue of the person

and voice among the buildings

you did not see informed

miles from the station long staves again

commonplace your glance running

what or how or why mouths

enclosed by a fence at the end of speech

if you want me to speak to you in Belgium I can

unsighted or something

going to stick at the edge of memory

missed by a fraction you think all you feel is tired

telling those people who take the flashes

only travel 15 feet a fraction

to get that shy boy to work hard believe in himself

and so from the beginning my philosophy wasn't to change anything

but to improve fully what was already there a fraction

changing the chemistry of the entire group

the one with the photograph even more specific

percentages at the moment just wide

a quiet town on the Baltic coast

the line concerned with the call

opposite the way down how the pause

was selected for its foreign

consonants balanced

by one who speaks of the point between eyes

thinking what she asked about coffee

after he approached the table

how my voice dropped

somewhere near hers the mother

I can imagine at breakfast whose features

addressed to the singular of teeth

the way vowels slap the boy

without reason how

the other person is himself

diminutive looking just to be found

you could drive to LA tonight and not fall asleep
playing close to home and you like it
giving next to nothing away
when you let the shoulder drop too soon
throw your arm in the air and say I don't believe it
the ground controlling the trend of the point
angry young men who are walking around
a couple of Italians and a Czech who live in Switzerland
usually only to shake hands and pick up the check
say I don't see it you didn't see it
the mental edge you have
dead solid even
you know it's flash photography again say
you want to hear it was out

at 6'4" you get into all sorts of trouble

which is one of the surprises

of words in German

in the air for the first time

asking if you can have some shade too

as the wind whips through your hair your shirt

under these conditions a foreign statement

tactically a bad mistake

to look at the sun

in your eyes less than you think

a surface of old tires

ankles and knees on the tarpaulin

just behind you the microphone

disappearing into the years

those were the days they used to flip a coin
in the spring on the slow red clay
between Sweden and Germany
and again only just
that the feeling is calming sensible
when it shows he's willing to take a chance
to come up with exactly what he needs
to look Madison Square Garden
with his arm still down
not a disaster war not broken out
in the air enough to curve
the crowd getting in on the act of calling lines
the idea the sense that by saying it
continues to apply pressure

who said you can't repeat

one or two mistakes

in situations like this getting back

to a scene you've seen over and over nice shoes

though you don't have enough leg to hold up your socks

when you're given the lane to run in mistakes

when the shovel hits you in the back

to name a city in Nebraska

the way you feel the way you think

to watch how everyone moves at the same time

when you're standing in line reading

the half you want to survive

as hits of water

just for the taste of it

one running out of his socks
six out of seven out of eight
instead of a finger in the eye
mine spelled "m-i-n-e"
nine minutes to go
in Pacific and Mountain Time
motion in a game of coordinates
place with vision a story
to make a spin move
the line it doesn't seem to have
speed to believe in a fighter who takes a punch
coming up with ideas the pad on his elbow
as if the film were speeded up
whether he hears the whistle or not

not a happy man as you can tell

whenever he's pulled together enough to scream

miles per hour what a wonderful touch

he used to be able to swing

taste after taste

two weeks after Frankfurt a direct attempt

trying to recollect himself two hours away by car

faces one more ball most people can't see

instead of one more peak diffused

if his name were on his back

how expressive misses are

to walking away how he must feel

just off the freeway Paris

left or right so it's not just the speed

first the story of the field no injuries
driving on the freeway running into a brick wall
says something about colder weather
active is always talking about the match
of things he thinks looks like a diseased area
when he smiles puts his arm around you
running at him someone was saying
penetration the pressure at the end of return
guarantees it's over steps up
wanting to let me speak
his scheme to go after people
didn't hold him knocked him down
too soon barely his own man
what he lives for not going to shave

to get the shoulder exactly right
he allows himself a fraction of a bounce
off the light green surface
striding like a colossus
watching a clinic doing everything better
gets to something you say the zone
you don't think you miss
how his right hand going into his left
tries to guess a wide open court
captured in a bottle
the title means more than
starting to practice rather than play
the game in your pocket catching
what no snapshot camera can

great lighting no wind no weather
between the knee and the hip
as quick as you are
breaks banks angles English
you realize is a woman with a small child
asking for trouble attacking the photographer
pulled up like a Mercedes
perfectly executed on that occasion
both his strength and frustration of late
a fiery temperament cramping again
technically and tactically
stating I've always wanted to be in this position
when he said please take your time
I am a father of three

capable of blasting you back to the stone age
one son would be enough luxury
40 times prior to the shot he hit
back into the seats somewhere in St. Louis
a situation in which sainthood was almost conferred
will host the event Sunday at two o'clock
swinging for something beyond the sign
time has been called running
everywhere behind you
back to second the wind taken
out of the sails your fingers crossed
along these lines nothing to be ashamed of
winning becomes a habit two pitches
two outs the crowd standing

it is 1959 the Dodgers are about to clinch
all scores together in the cabinet facing these files
she barely hears him the complete body of husbands
why should she expect an explanation a portrait
of Mr. B a crate the old men unloaded
in the only words she heard used to describe it
the ship in French the Alabama wolf in a hotel around the corner
from the club a portrait of Lady Hester in a tough place
as someone puts a hand to mouth across the continent
awakening the desert the piano player longs for
Shelley's poems on Crusoe's Island in Latin
a thousand miles up the Amazon
headhunter country the wreck of a car
slumps in the dry grass the world is round

feinting to the right arm under your head

the game's deep patterns sunlight

uncoiling like some small

state of being the crowd meant to stop

without illusion the hope of a line drive rising

to the wall halfway through October

off balance not seeing

it stop what the place called

cars pulled off the road the afternoon designed

to think ahead because it was meant to

describe the physics of an arc

the ball describes

skimming into the green deep

the anchor bites to leave for a moment home

another scene the more you think about the door
with a motion everyone looks directly at
a fraction of a second a face when you hear
I'm tired again her every gesture
the one next to apparently
a favorite dish the first time in years
you undress slowly take the arm you remember
waiting outside for some reason reach the window
close to yours the one at the foot
of the stairs hand with a key
you tell yourself as if permitting
the power of a knife and fork to look
satisfied and recognized so easy
to wake up moving in the middle of the room

morning in Latin angle twists
beyond the horizon less
among the chickens in the coop
to be named wire drying his open wings
when he sees the one who takes part
in the wind about him measures
the idea in the yard about the house
at seven o'clock lifts his eyes
according to the neighbor who asked
the difference between the stars
in Portuguese in a dialect
he understands in less
than a week sunlight rising
noticed as fatigue turns to sleep

the next day dead calm

looks at the shapes of nature the soft lines

you try to keep abreast of the issues

which take you back minutes

the last few months have been filled with

the only letters you care about ones that spell

enough said of waking the moment clouds

follow if you will quickly

your head in a noose

on the tips of your toes arching

your back as much as possible overcast quiet

please the domino effect fatigue

something physical

you expect at the end of the day

traces a nervous system in plants

from the moment of his intention to injure the vegetable

working the iodine down into the puncture

was a stunning claim

much of it randomly difficult

ranging from an egg to his own cat

action or indeed real signals

inside the cell imbalance across the membrane

radishes to be ripped apart the result

to propagate from cell to cell

forces the tendril over

work a fast-acting hormone

yards of chart recordings later

on our way little plants on our way

when you're in the car and moving
to get as close as you can
to Queens the answer will come a year from now
from the angle you're watching in a chair
for two reasons a pendulum swing
whether you sneeze or not
what is there to say
getting lighter and lighter on your feet
four countries on two continents
handcuffed because you dress in your name
and speak as though you have unshakable confidence
leaving the house at 4:30 each morning
in a perfect circle
how many bullets can you dodge

something he had expected as it now happens

talking about parental discretion

advised an opposite

reaction which makes him want to warm up

and is only going to keep getting worse which

evidently hurts being seldom injured

talking American language

with you once

again a surprising number of people

you think the thing to look for by the way

in Yackandandah Maroochydora Cobrawanga Oodnadatta

or the Alligator Billabong near Darwin

which clarifies once

there doesn't appear to be wind

sometimes dissonant sounds voices in the room
the norm in an unreconstructed world
civilized less inhabited
by the body we live in than scratch
salt chasm not white Beethoven Coltrane
reflected in what one wants of the knowledge
one is to absorb as a single person
having left the trail of tears
in Memphis thinking made visible in ways
content in quilted strips in a color scheme the family
talking to an outsider labels chaos rhythms
the democracy of each musician
listening to the other who speaks
of exclusion at the margins of what we mean

say the voice able to sustain the note

as the reader is told again

and again prompted

soon after news of his death reaches England mosaics

inlaid on walls and the pavement elsewhere

set off by coincidence in prose

appearing in books making

his life seem like an ordinary life

using needles to knit a shirt in the language

of gesture abandoned

birds that live in water

speak now to answer yes or no

sometimes elliptical at second or third hand

sometimes in writing as in speech

take the parable of the loaves and fishes
if progress always comes too late
for what is a soldier next to the daughter of a king
under the balcony tears streaming from his eyes
in wind and rain he was always there
not giving in to nostalgia
when she wanted to see him
worse than rabbits like playing the lottery
sometimes you listen and the house is full of people
whether you talk or not all hell breaking loose
no strength to sleep though you want to
shoot first think later
music music
a moment before you close your eyes

in the place we visit the landscape

flooding back to be touched

in search of examples

as shadow and light thinking the quirks

the presence of a subject caused to frame perhaps

what happens the instant the object gives

an image that is also a thing

in a sense threads

above all pictured as the birds flew down

to the camera if only because of the difference

light in the distance and the reflection

recognized as the arm

rests in a frame that frames the world

as if it were a picture

as she did so the whole figure turned
in the middle of the room said
how it happened the jacket
let slip looking an hour later
at the crowd of people he didn't know
why another view of the coat
on the other hand placed
possibly on his bed
in the act of taking off her shoes
while behind him emotion coming to pieces
as it came back into the room feeling
as it reflected wonderful
conversation looking about to think
of something to do at the door

two heroes we are told as if to rhyme

what he can't get out of his head

facing east writing by hand in his native tongue

to distinguish between the things he saw

a long nose and high cheekbones

the face a thin white lie

you forget in detail reading it twice

the drift of thought argument at that level

suspended in the sky above a landscape

understanding in a better sense

the disappearance of rocks

makes her promise an illusion

he returned to in thinking word for word

not counting glosses and the like

the spaces filled exactly without accents
as he was leaving the house
words and gestures for a week or so
before he turned and with a deep bow said
I wanted nothing better than to check them myself
asking him would it be possible telling her to stay
where she was in the dark
mosaic on top of some other notes
before she came back to the place she was going
saying she had had a telegram telling her to go home
rather halfheartedly before the next page
punctuated by hypotheses say
sighs excuses silences the language
will look like I have finished

STEPHEN RATCLIFFE wrote these 14-line poems in the 1980s in Bolinas California, where he has lived since 1973.

www.ingramcontent.com/pod-product-compliance
Lightning Source LLC
Chambersburg PA
CBHW081755100526
44592CB00015B/2440